JAY HONDRO

Make Healthy Eating Fun!

A Quick Guide for Parents Wanting Healthy Eating Kids

Copyright © 2024 by Jay Hondro

All rights reserved. No part of this publication may be reproduced, stored or transmitted in any form or by any means, electronic, mechanical, photocopying, recording, scanning, or otherwise without written permission from the publisher. It is illegal to copy this book, post it to a website, or distribute it by any other means without permission.

Jay Hondro asserts the moral right to be identified as the author of this work.

Jay Hondro has no responsibility for the persistence or accuracy of URLs for external or third-party Internet Websites referred to in this publication and does not guarantee that any content on such Websites is, or will remain, accurate or appropriate.

Designations used by companies to distinguish their products are often claimed as trademarks. All brand names and product names used in this book and on its cover are trade names, service marks, trademarks and registered trademarks of their respective owners. The publishers and the book are not associated with any product or vendor mentioned in this book. None of the companies referenced within the book have endorsed the book.

First edition

This book was professionally typeset on Reedsy.
Find out more at reedsy.com

"Do the best you can until you know better.
Then when you know better, do better."

MAYA ANGELOU

Contents

1 Introduction 1
2 Understanding the Foundations of Nutrition 3
3 Food Groups, Suggested Intake, and H2O 12
4 Navigating Traps and Making Food Fun! 19
5 Tackling the Challenges of Picky Eating 26
6 Conclusion: Celebrating Our Roles as Parents 30

1

Introduction

Step into the realm of crisp carrots, succulent apples, and the delightful journey of nurturing wholesome eating habits in your little ones. Ha ha, not really! Crisp carrots and succulent apples are tasty, but let's face it, making healthy choices is tough. It's even tougher when we have kids and do our best to navigate through our busy lives. This guide will be a journey, but not a journey of telling you that wholesome eating is simple and without its challenges. Instead, we're going to focus on educating ourselves about nutrition, learning how to make healthier choices, and most importantly, how to involve our children in making healthy eating fun!

Within this guide, we'll embark on the rainbow of possibilities that come with making healthy choices a joyful part of your family's daily routine. We'll discuss some of the basics of nutrition and how even the dietary decisions we make as parents impact our little ones from birth through adolescence. We'll uncover the profound influence these choices can have, not only on your child's well-being but also on their lasting connection with food. Parenthood is a wild ride, and steering through the mazes of mealtime can bring its ups and downs. You're not alone out here though! From the allure of sugary snacks to the

MAKE HEALTHY EATING FUN!

constant battle with broccoli, we get it. We'll unravel the challenges parents face and equip you with the tools to turn mealtime madness into a masterpiece. Get ready for practical tips, a sprinkle of humor, and strategies to turn your little ones into healthy eating champions!

By the end of "Make Healthy Eating Fun," you will have gained a better grasp of nutrition as well as useful tools and techniques for providing a fun and diverse way of making food interesting and entertaining!

Remember, it's not just about what's on the plate; it's about the joy, laughter, and love that come with it. Happy munching!

2

Understanding the Foundations of Nutrition

Parenthood is a journey of constant learning and at the heart of the journey lies the intricate world of childhood nutrition. In this chapter, we will dive into the foundations of nutrition, the essential nutrients crucial for development and growth, the significance of diverse food groups, and practical guidelines for suggested daily consumption. Don't worry, the boring stuff is at the beginning but trust me it gets better!

Look at Nutrition from a Whole-Food Perspective!

Nutrition is not merely about sustenance; it is a dynamic interplay of elements that shapes a child's physical and cognitive development. Remember, each of these elements is a building block for your child's nutritional structure.

Let's start understanding this structure by talking about macronutrients.

What are macronutrients, you ask?

Well, macronutrients are **The Pillars of Energy and Growth!**

They are the proteins, carbohydrates, and fats that are all the cornerstones of a balanced diet. Proteins support growth, carbohydrates provide energy, and fats aid in brain development. Understanding this balance is pivotal for laying the groundwork for a child's overall well-being. Let's take a little deeper look at our child's use of each of these macronutrients as they develop from cradle through adolescence and how they should be introduced

Proteins: These quite literally are the building blocks for our bodies! Protein is necessary for a wide range of bodily functions, including the healing and maintenance of tissues found in the muscles (skin, organs, blood, hair, and nails). The body can manufacture 11 of the 20 amino acids that make up protein; the remaining nine must be obtained from diet.

How do they affect our kids?

Early Years (0-2 years):

- Infants rely on breast milk or formula for protein needs, crucial for rapid growth.
- **As solids are introduced, include pureed meats, eggs, and dairy for a protein boost.**

Preschool (3-5 years):

- Proteins continue supporting muscle development and overall growth.
- **Diversify sources with lean meats, poultry, fish, legumes, and**

dairy.

School Age (6-12 years):

- Balanced protein intake aids ongoing growth and development.
- **Introduce variety with lean meats, plant-based proteins, and dairy.**

Adolescence (13-18 years):

- Protein becomes essential for puberty-related growth spurts.
- **Encourage a mix of lean meats, dairy, plant-based proteins, and whole grains.**

Carbohydrates: The body uses carbohydrates as its primary and most accessible energy source. For both children and adults, they are an essential component of a nutritious diet. The two primary types of carbohydrates are simple sugars, or carbs, such as fructose, glucose, and lactose, which are also present in nutritious whole fruits.

Take a look at the way carbs impact...

Early Years (0-2 years):

- Breast milk or formula provides primary carbohydrate sources.
- Introduce whole grains, fruits, and veggies with complementary foods.

Preschool (3-5 years):

- Carbohydrates support energy for active play and brain development.
- Emphasize complex carbs from whole grains, fruits, and veggies.

School Age (6-12 years):

- Sustaining energy for increased cognitive demands and activities.
- Balance with complex carbs and limit refined sugars.

Adolescence (13-18 years):

- Meeting energy needs for growth spurts and increased activities.

- Encourage a mix of complex carbs for sustained energy.

Fats: In addition to providing the body with fuel, fats aid in the absorption of fat-soluble vitamins (such as A, D, E, and K), which the body can only absorb when fat is present in the diet. Consuming adequate good fats is crucial for development and growth!

We've all heard of *good fat* vs *bad fat* right? Check this out...

Early Years (0-2 years):

- Fats in breast milk or formula are crucial for brain development.
- **Introduce healthy fats like avocados and nut butters.**

Preschool (3-5 years):

- Fats support brain function and energy storage.
- **Include healthy fats from nuts, seeds, and fish.**

School Age (6-12 years):

- Balanced fats for overall health and well-being.
- **Really focus on good fats in this phase like different varieties of nuts, vegetable oils, oily fish, soy products, and green leafy vegetables. Stay away from bad fats like those found in meals with lots of butter, cream, biscuits, chips, and saturated and trans fats!**

Adolescence (13-18 years):

- Believe it or not fats play a role in hormonal balance during puberty. Fat cells produce the hormone leptin, which is believed to tell the body it has enough energy stored up to start the growth spurt and other puberty-related changes.
- **So...continue to stay away from those bad fats and if we start them young, by this time we'll be happy we did! Puberty and teenage years are a whole different parent guide haha!**

In essence, adapting macronutrient intake for your child's growth is an ongoing process. It's about providing the right balance at the right time while embracing the diversity of a well-rounded diet. Tailoring macronutrients isn't just a practical step; it's our guide to fostering a healthy and vibrant future.

So now that we've talked about macronutrients, let's explore micronutrients and how they impact our children's everyday lives.

Micronutrients: The Unsung Heroes of Health

Vitamins and minerals, often referred to as micronutrients, play a subtle yet indispensable role in maintaining optimal health. From bone development to immune function, these tiny powerhouses contribute to the intricate dance of physiological processes.

Vitamins are the Catalysts for Vital Functions

Vitamin A:

- Essential for vision, vitamin A supports the health of the eyes and

is integral to the immune system.
- Found in carrots, sweet potatoes, and leafy greens, it ensures proper functioning of the eyes and promotes immune resilience.

Vitamin C:

- Renowned for its immune-boosting properties, vitamin C also aids in collagen synthesis, promoting skin health.
- Abundant in citrus fruits, strawberries, and bell peppers, it contributes to tissue repair and protection against infections.

Vitamin D:

- Vital for bone health, vitamin D facilitates the absorption of calcium and phosphorus.
- Sun exposure, fatty fish, and fortified dairy products are sources that support skeletal development and overall well-being.

Vitamin K:

- Essential for blood clotting and bone metabolism, vitamin K plays a crucial role in wound healing.
- Leafy greens, broccoli, and soybeans are rich sources that contribute to proper blood coagulation and bone health.

Vitamin E:

- A potent antioxidant, vitamin E protects cells from oxidative stress and supports skin health.
- Nuts, seeds, and spinach are sources that contribute to cellular protection and overall antioxidant defense.

Minerals are the Building Blocks for Health

Calcium:

- Found in dairy products, leafy greens, and fortified foods, calcium is crucial for bone and teeth formation.
- It plays a pivotal role in muscle function, nerve transmission, and blood clotting.

Iron:

- Essential for oxygen transport in the blood, iron is found in red meat, legumes, and fortified cereals.
- Adequate iron intake prevents anemia and supports cognitive function and immune response.

Zinc:

- A trace mineral with significant implications for immune function and wound healing.
- Found in meat, dairy, and legumes, zinc contributes to immune resilience and cellular repair.

Magnesium:

- Vital for muscle and nerve function, magnesium is present in whole grains, nuts, and leafy greens.
- It supports energy production, muscle relaxation, and the maintenance of a healthy heartbeat.

Potassium:

- Critical for maintaining fluid balance, potassium is abundant in bananas, oranges, and potatoes.
- It supports heart health, aids in muscle contraction, and regulates blood pressure.

Try to think about micronutrients like the conductor of a symphony. They ensure a harmonious balance in the intricate orchestra of our health. Their roles extend beyond individual processes, intertwining in a complex dance that sustains life. As parents and caretakers, understanding the importance of these tiny powerhouses equips us with the knowledge to nourish our families for a resilient and thriving future. Through diverse and balanced meals, we provide the right use of instruments to harmonize bone health, immune function, cellular protection, and the overall vitality of our loved ones.

3

Food Groups, Suggested Intake, and H2O

I know we just had a lot of nutrition information and I promise the facts and bullet points are almost done. Hang in there, it'll be worth it I promise! Before we get to the practical tips and tricks, I wanted to quickly touch on some key points on food groups and caloric intake. So here we go...

Fruits and Vegetables: Nutrient Treasure Chest
Fruits and vegetables are nature's nutrient treasure trove, providing an array of vitamins, minerals, and antioxidants. Grasping the importance of incorporating these colorful components into the diet is essential for optimal health.

Guidance: Encourage a varied intake of fruits and vegetables, emphasizing different colors for diverse nutrient profiles. Foster a love for fresh produce as a regular part of meals.

Whole Grains: The Sustaining Force of Complex Carbohydrates
Whole grains stand as the sustaining force of complex carbohydrates, offering sustained energy and essential fiber. Appreciating the role of

whole grains in supporting digestion and energy levels is crucial for balanced nutrition.

Guidance: Opt for whole grain options such as brown rice, whole wheat bread, and oats. Explore the benefits of incorporating diverse grains into the child's diet.

Dairy and Alternatives: Nurture Bone Health

Dairy and dairy alternatives play a crucial role in nurturing bone health through the provision of calcium and vitamin D. Understanding the significance of these sources ensures the foundation for strong bones and teeth.

Guidance: Integrate dairy or suitable alternatives into the diet, ensuring a balance between calcium intake and dietary preferences. Explore fortified options for added nutritional value.

Don't worry, we're almost done with the boring stuff but it's very important to look at suggested intake. Healthy choices and portion control will always go hand in hand.

Suggested Daily Consumption

Understanding a child's caloric needs is akin to tailoring a garment to fit perfectly. Recognizing the variations in energy requirements during different growth phases is essential for maintaining a healthy weight and supporting development.

Caloric Needs: Tailoring Intake to Growth Phases

Children's demands for calories vary according to age, gender, activity level, and personal growth patterns. It's crucial to remember that these are only recommendations; specific needs may vary. Children's daily recommended calorie intake is frequently given in a range. The approximate calorie requirements for each age group are as follows:

Toddlers (1-3 years): Caloric Range (1000-1400 calories per day)
Toddlers need enough calories to sustain their play and exploration because they are active learners.

Nutrient-Dense Diet: For a well-rounded diet, promote a range of vibrant fruits and vegetables, whole grains, dairy products, and dairy substitutes. Nutrient-dense snacks promote healthy eating habits from a young age.

Preschoolers (4-5 years): Caloric Range (1200-1800 calories per day)
Preschoolers' calorie requirements rise as they become increasingly self-sufficient in order to sustain their developing bodies. Promote a variety of nutritious grains, lean meats, and a rainbow of fruits and vegetables.

Balanced Nutrition: To foster a positive relationship with food, teach portion control. A favorable attitude toward nutrition can be fostered by involving children in the planning and preparation of meals.

School-Age Children (6-10 years): Caloric Range (1600-2200 calories per day)
Increased calorie requirements result from participation in extracurricular activities and school. Stress the need to eat a balanced diet and the many nutritional benefits of eating different food types.

Active Lifestyle: Encourage youngsters to engage in physical activities they enjoy as part of a healthy and active lifestyle. Teach children to recognize the value of nutrients and to choose food with awareness.

Preteens and Teens (11-18 years): Caloric Range (1700-2400 calories for girls and 2000-3000 calories for boys per day)
   Significant growth spurts during puberty have an effect on caloric needs. The emphasis should be on eating a diet that is well-balanced and rich in the necessary vitamins, minerals, healthy fats, carbs, and proteins.

Option Dense in Nutrients: As their dietary choices become more independent, point them in the direction of wholesome choices. Stress the value of preserving a positive body image and choosing foods that promote general health.

Now, one of the most important things you will read in this guide is...

HYDRATION! HYDRATION! HYDRATION!
   I would not be doing anyone justice if I didn't save the best for last! And yes, I might have yelled it. As parents, we need to ensure our children are drinking plenty of water, and emphasize that it should be everyone's beverage of choice. Here are the key factors and why this is so important:

Maximizes Physical Performance:

- Helps Sustain Energy Levels: Water is necessary to keep hydration at its best, which has a direct impact on energy levels. Fatigue brought on by dehydration has an affect on a child's focus and performance during physical activity.
- Cognitive Function: Attention, memory, and problem-solving abilities are all supported by adequate hydration. Better learning outcomes and academic performance are correlated with staying

hydrated.

Regulates Temperature:

- Overheating: Sports and physical play are common activities for kids and teenagers. By encouraging perspiration, avoiding overheating, and lowering the risk of heat-related disorders during physical activity, water helps control body temperature.

Transports and Absorbs Nutrients:

- Encourages Nutrient Transport: Water plays a critical role in the body's transportation of nutrients. It promotes general growth and development by assisting in the distribution and absorption of vital nutrients from the digestive system to different cells..

Promotes Joint and Muscle Health:

- Physical Growth: Drinking enough water is crucial for the well-being of your muscles and joints. Maintaining joint lubrication lowers the chance of injuries during physical activity and promotes healthy bone and muscle growth.

Helps Regulate Digestive Health:

- Prevent Constipation: Keeping the digestive system healthy requires drinking plenty of water. In addition to encouraging regular bowel movements and a healthy gastrointestinal tract, it helps soften stool and avoid constipation.

Aids in Kidney Function:

- Kidney Health: The health of the kidneys depends on enough water. Water supports the kidneys in keeping a healthy balance of fluids and electrolytes by assisting the body in eliminating waste and toxins through urine.

Essential for Dental Health:

- Minimizes Oral Health Problems: Having a healthy mouth is facilitated by drinking water, particularly fluoridated water. It acts as a mouthwash, neutralizes acids, and lowers the chance of cavities and tooth decay.

Assists in Weight Management:

- Encourages a Healthy Weight: Water can be an excellent substitute for sugary beverages as it has no calories. Promoting water intake can help people control their weight healthily and cut back on sugar intake, which is linked to a number of health problems.

Helps Cope with Growth Spurts:

- Fulfills Increasing Needs: The body requires more water during times of fast growth, such as puberty. The extra demands that growth spurts make on the body are supported by maintaining adequate water.

Establishes Healthy Habits:

- Develops Healthy Hydration Habits: Promoting consistent water consumption from an early age helps create hydration habits that are beneficial throughout adolescence and maturity. It promotes mindful eating habits by assisting kids in telling the difference between hunger and thirst.

Wow, that was a lot of information! It may seem a bit overwhelming, but it's so important to understand the importance of fueling our bodies effectively. After all, our children's general health, development, and well-being are fundamentally dependent on getting enough water. Ensuring that children have access to clean and safe water throughout the day is a critical responsibility of parents and other caregivers.

4

Navigating Traps and Making Food Fun!

Parenting is hard…it's really hard! Our busy schedules and complex lives play such a key factor on how we go about feeding our kids. In this chapter, we're going to break down some of the bad traps we often fall into, and dive into some helpful tips to transform the way we think about the way food fuels our kids. We're going to discuss overindulging in food, relying on processed foods, and how we are setting a not-so-good example for our children. Sounds like a lot of negativity, but I promise we'll focus more on how to transform those negatives into fun and positive outcomes.

There are a lot of factors that go into why our society tends to overindulge in food but don't worry there are no judgments here. Remember, our focus in this guide is to understand those factors and establish healthy habits! Let's take a look at some of the main factors in overindulgence:

Societal Norms and Pressures:

Our choices about food as parents are greatly influenced by the larger social environment. The urge to serve abundant meals and a variety of goodies can be felt in a culture where plenty is frequently associated with kindness and care. It takes deliberate effort to rethink the ideals we identify with food and parenting in order to deviate from these conventions.

Comfort and Emotional Nourishment:

Loaded with sentimental value, food serves as a means of celebration, solace, and bonding within our families. Food and emotions are linked when a loved one serves a favorite meal or offers a sweet treat to ease a child's emotional pain. This emotional bond may unintentionally cause us to overindulge in our desire to care for their hearts as well as their bodies.

Family Traditions and Generational Influences:

Our parenting style bears the echoes of our own upbringing and family traditions. Family members with good intentions might suggest having seconds or providing sweet treats, stressing that having plenty is a sign of family support. Redefining food's place in our family's story while honoring the ethnic diversity it contributes is a necessary step in unraveling these generational influences.

Sweets as Prizes:

Treats are frequently used as rewards in parenting because it's believed that these indulgences provide happiness and positive reinforcement.

But this connection may unintentionally foster a belief system in which particular foods are associated with success or approval. It takes imagination and a change of viewpoint to find other, non-food-based methods to celebrate achievements.

Outside Pressure:

It's a special struggle to navigate the outside pressures from playdates, social gatherings, and well-intentioned advice. Clear communication and a strong commitment to our family's nutritional values are necessary to strike a balance between our children's desire to participate in shared experiences and our dedication to healthy eating.

Lack of Nutrition Education:

In a world where there is an abundance of contradicting information regarding eating, making poor decisions can be attributed to a lack of thorough nutrition education. But don't worry, we talked about that in chapter 1, so you are way ahead of the curve.

Time, Time, and More Time:

Schedules are often hectic in modern life, leaving little time for food preparation and planning. Eating out or going for quick, processed food can seem like sensible solutions, but they can also be alluring. It takes deliberate decision-making and a dedication to setting aside time for healthful meals to strike a balance between convenience and nutritional content.

So, how do we turn these negative factors into positive fun and

nutrition? And how do we avoid the constant fast food trips and reliance on processed foods? Finally, how do we set a good example?

Well, we start with a plan and an awareness of our choices. We start to look at food as an opportunity to grow closer to our kids. Not by making food a focal point in our relationship by any means, but by involving our children in food decisions from a young age. A study that was published in the "International Journal of Behavioral Nutrition and Physical Activity" found that including children in the process of preparing meals is connected with improved dietary habits. The likelihood of children selecting and consuming healthier foods was increased when they participated in cooking activities. So let's get to the fun stuff and I'll give some examples on how we can do this.

Start a Conversation About Food: Be Open to Communication: Create an atmosphere where kids can talk freely about how they feel about eating. Let them share their likes, dislikes, and any queries they may have. Give them a chance to open up on why they may think a certain food is "gross" or "yucky".

Actively Listen: Pay attention to what your child has to say about food without passing judgment. This promotes mutual trust and facilitates group decision-making around meals.

Establish an Independent Mindset: Construct a "Healthy Choices" Area: Arrange a section of the kitchen or pantry and stock it with wholesome snack alternatives. Let kids select their own snacks to give them a sense of independence in selecting wholesome options.

Teach Portion Control: Assist kids in comprehending the appropriate size of portions. To illustrate proper serving sizes, use visual aids like miniature containers or hand measurements.

Provide a Balanced Habit Model: Set an Example: Kids pick up knowledge through observation. Show off your appreciation for a range of foods, exhibit balanced eating practices, and express gratitude for the sustenance they bring.

Communicate Your Joy in Making Healthier Food Choices: Share your happiness and contentment in choosing healthy foods. Talk about how eating a healthy diet gives you energy and improves your general well-being.

Make Nutrition Instruction Fun: Interactive Learning: Create interactive classes that incorporate nutrition instruction. Play games, tell stories, or conduct experiments to educate kids the value of a well-balanced diet and the advantages of various food categories.

Scavenger hunts in grocery stores: Turn grocery shopping into an adventure. Make a list of foods that are healthy and set a challenge for kids to identify and research each one.

Promote Mindful Eating Habits: Sensory Exploration: Motivate your kids to use their senses when they're eating. Talk about the tastes, textures, and colors of various foods to encourage awareness and gratitude for the food they eat.

Savor and Satisfy: Teaching kids to chew deeply and appreciate the flavor of each meal will help them learn to savor every bite. This discourages mindless overeating and encourages a sense of fullness.

MAKE HEALTHY EATING FUN!

Establish a Happy Eating Environment: **Design a Vibrant Color Scheme:** Increase the visual attractiveness of meals by adding a range of vibrant fruits and vegetables. Kids may help choose colorful vegetables when they go grocery shopping.

Family Cooking Adventures: Involve your family in the food preparation process. Encourage kids to participate in age-appropriate cooking activities to help them feel proud of and connected to their food.

Promote Healthful Festivities: **Activity-Based Festivities:** Move the celebration's emphasis from the cuisine to something else. Instead of depending just on candy to make important events memorable, arrange games, outdoor excursions, or artistic endeavors.

Nutrient-Rich Party Snacks: When desserts are served during festivities, pair them with nutrient-dense foods like yogurt parfaits, fruit skewers, or whole-grain snacks.

Eliminate Screen Time During Meals: **Focused Dining:** Make sure everyone is "Present" when it comes to mealtime. Put those phones, iPads, or other little distractions away and really engage with each other.

Screen Free Zone: The restriction of screen time helps to ensure that everyone can converse and interact distraction-free!

Consider Treats as Spoken Pleasures: Set aside particular days to indulge in decadent treats. This emphasizes moderation and lessens the appeal of regular indulgence by helping kids identify such sweets on rare occasions.

Handmade Delights: Try making your own renditions of your favorite

NAVIGATING TRAPS AND MAKING FOOD FUN!

sweets. This gives you control over the ingredients and makes for a great bonding activity.

As you can see, there are so many ways to start involving your kids in food and making healthy choices fun. Do me a favor, take a little time after reading this guide, and start mapping out a plan or a roadmap, if you will, on how you'll start your own journey. It doesn't have to be robust or life-changing but start by picking one of the ideas above and implementing it this week. You'll be surprised at how responsive your kids will be if they see that you're excited about it too!

5

Tackling the Challenges of Picky Eating

Ok, I saved the very best for last and I would be remiss if I didn't touch on every parent's challenge at one time or another…"How do I deal with my picky-eating child?" Trust me, we all have either had a kid who seems to dislike anything and everything will only eat hot dogs or chicken tenders, or loves everything candy and sweets and refuses to eat actual "food". I could write an entire book on picky eating and still not address the issue fully, but I think the most important thing to understand is that it is perfectly normal. Here are my top 10 reasons for picky eating and some tips on how to deal with them…

1. **Normal Development:** Picky eating is often a common phase in a child's development as they assert independence and explore preferences.

Strategy: This one is what it is folks. It's perfectly normal and will continue to be normal until the end of time. Acknowledge the refusal calmly and try to avoid acting frustrated, as this can create a negative association with food. Keep reinforcing that everyone has different tastes, and it's okay to have preferences. The faster we can accept it's going to happen the easier it is to move on and have a plan to deal with it.

2. **Sensory Factors:** Many children have increased sensitivities to certain tastes, textures, and smells, making them more selective about the foods they eat.

Strategy: Gradually introduce foods with different textures. Incorporate both crunchy and smooth textures to help children become more accustomed. It's ok to let your kids taste, nibble, and sometimes spit out different foods as you introduce new things. Control the environment and the right time by making it educational. Explain to them where the food might have come from or from what animal or plant. Have them guess the food and make it ok for them not to like something while encouraging them to at least try it.

3. **Wanting Control:** Children often want to feel in control and assert autonomy in their environment leading to picky eating and often food tantrums.

*Strategy: Offer some choices within reasonable limits. Allow them to select between two options, providing a sense of autonomy without overwhelming decisions. Encourage them to express their preferences and discuss the reasons behind their choices. Help them to feel **they** made the choice and you'll be surprised how their attitude changes.*

4. **Fear of New Foods(Neophobia):** The fear of new or unfamiliar foods is a real phobia and is often experienced by children of all ages.

Strategy: Familiarize and allow the introduction of new foods outside of mealtime. Encourage exploration through touch, smell, and other sensory experiences. Use storytelling or educational activities to make the unknown more familiar. Try to relate a time when you were a kid and tried something

MAKE HEALTHY EATING FUN!

new and you loved it!

5. **Routine:** Children may seek comfort in routine and familiarity, preferring familiar foods over new or unfamiliar ones.

Strategy: Acknowledge and praise any willingness to try new foods. Celebrate small victories to build confidence and encourage continued exploration. Create a "tasting journal" to document their achievements.

6. **Negative Food Experiences:** Negative incidents like choking or food poisoning can create aversions and contribute to picky eating.

Strategy: Start by explaining the importance of chewing your food and even turning it into a simple game of counting to a certain number (can you believe 32 chews is the recommended number? Unless it's softer food like mashed potatoes where 5 to 10 times is recommended). Secondly, try replacing the negative food item with a very similar food item and slowly begin to gain the trust back in that particular food.

7. **Genetic Factors or Inherited Traits:** Genetics can play a role in determining a child's predisposition to certain tastes and textures, influencing their eating habits.

Strategy: Take the time to learn exactly what foods your child might have a dislike or sour taste for. It's ok for them to talk about it and you may find that you also don't like those same foods for the same reasons. Once you form a common bond good or bad with food, you'll notice it sparks a better conversation around mealtime. Encourage them to express what alternatives they would prefer.

8. **Environmental Influences:** Modeling Behavior: Children mimic

the eating behaviors of their parents or caregivers, adopting similar food preferences and aversions.

Strategy: Serve meals family-style, allowing children to choose portions from shared dishes. This promotes a communal and inclusive dining experience. Identify any cultural or family history significance of the dishes on the table.

9. **Peer Pressure:** Social dynamics, such as pressure from peers or exposure to other picky eaters, can influence a child's food choices.

Strategy: Let your child provide alternative options when faced with or around other picky eaters. They may feel the need to act out when around other kids, but if you empower them to make a decision for themselves their mind becomes more positive. Provide assistance by offering a substitute that aligns with their preferences while still meeting nutritional needs. Encourage them to express what alternatives they would prefer.

10. **Mealtime Atmosphere:** If a mealtime is often tense or uncomfortable for a child, it could quite often lead to a reluctance to food or wanting to eat at certain times.

Strategy: Last, but certainly not least, and one of my most important factors... Children are very perceptive and they will always gravitate to places where they feel secure and the most free. When we make mealtime enjoyable and a place where we can talk and share, we teach our kids that food is wholesome and fun! On the other hand, if we use mealtime as a chance to complain about our day or gripe at our kids for not eating what's on their plate, they are going to be reluctant to eat and interact in a positive manner. Be mindful about your attitude during this time and use it as a positive space for your kids and the entire family.

6

Conclusion: Celebrating Our Roles as Parents

I hope you enjoyed this quick guide, and always remember that you are doing a great job as a parent! We all have busy lives and busy schedules between work, school, sports, dance, and every other extracurricular activity under the sun. Parenting is a never-ending adventure of personal development, resiliency, and love that knows no bounds. When it comes to your child and food, recognize the profound impact you have on shaping not just their eating habits but their lifelong relationship with food. Embrace the change that is occurring in your approach to parenting, keeping in mind that your ability to adapt is a demonstration of your dedication to the health and happiness of your child.

Remember to celebrate the journey! Think back on the things you've accomplished, the obstacles you've conquered, and the happy times you've spent with others around the table. Take pleasure in the little things that bring you joy, such as every mouthful of new food, every pleasant mealtime, and every occasion on which your child makes a healthy choice. Remember that learning new things about food can be

CONCLUSION: CELEBRATING OUR ROLES AS PARENTS

both educational and fun for both you and your child!

If you found this book enjoyable and helpful, please take the time to leave a review on Amazon. If you learned just one thing, I'm happy and feel like this guide was worth writing, so taking the time to leave a review will go a long way in helping me write future guides.

Made in the USA
Monee, IL
01 March 2024